Letters to the Rock

Letters to the Rock

A Spiritual Journey in Poetry

By
Leonie Phoenix

Illustrated by Leonie Phoenix

authorHOUSE®

AuthorHouse™
1663 Liberty Drive
Bloomington, IN 47403
www.authorhouse.com
Phone: 1-800-839-8640

Published by AuthorHouse   11/14/2012

ISBN: 978-1-4772-4625-2 (sc)
ISBN: 978-1-4772-4626-9 (e)

CONTENTS

Part One
Holding on to a Rock on Shifting Sands

Part Two
Words from the Depths of Sheol

Part Three
Healing and Peace

Part Four
Trust in the True Rock

PART ONE

Holding on to a Rock on Shifting Sands

A Whisper

Secure in my bed,
Between sleeping and waking,
One word was whispered . . . .

Glimpses

Laughter in eyes,
Gentleness in strength,
The kindness in a voice;
These simple things
Are glimpses of Heaven on earth,
Drifting in and out of the shore of consciousness.

Finding the Words

If only I could find the words to
Let you know how much I
offer my heart to
validate and
encourage you,
Yes, comfort and affirm, and never hurt,
offend or
undermine you.

Acceptance

An ancient Adonis from a bygone era,
A new-born lamb in a distant field,
A sun shining in the furthest skies;
Therefore,
Let me be content
That even the smallest of your rays
Should fall on me,
Shedding warmth on my soul.

Happily Deluded

A simple "Yes,
I will pray"
Gives me greater joy
Than I can express,

Reading into it more
Than was ever intended,
It's all I could want
or dare hope for.

Through the Wilderness

Through the wilderness
Of an ever changing will
Beats a steadfast heart

River

I most certainly respect
That, by far, superior intellect,
And can admire this physique,
Though neither is the end I seek.
I stand awe-struck by a special soul,
But even this is not the whole.
Here is where I end and start:
A river of love pours out from my heart.

Futile Efforts

She told me hard facts,
Hoping to turn me away,
But my heart softened.

B.S.

A whole new meaning
to the initials B.S.:
Beautiful Soul

Profound Soul

You are God's masterpiece
To be celebrated,
Not a mistake,
To be crossed out.

The Creator wants you to live
As the best version
Of the wonderful person
He made you to be.

Profound soul,
He made no mistakes in you,
You were especially
and exquisitely designed,
To serve and to love.

All He asks of you
Is to give Him the glory,
Remaining ever faithful to Him;
And though suffering now,
Eventually, you will
Radiate true joy.

An Apple?

I will not bring you
A single apple,
Firm and red, like that
Eve gave to Adam.

Not one fruit will pass
From my hand to yours,
To be devoured and
Discarded in minutes.

Accept instead, this tiny seed;
How fitting that it cannot grow
In this heated, hostile climate.

Keep it with you, dry and safe,
Until your travels take you
To an undiscovered land,
Where the soil is fertile and cool.

There you may plant it
And it will surely sprout
Something small and green,
Living, delicate,
And in need of care.

Nurture this small shoot,
From which your tree
Will shower you with
An abundance of fruit:
Harvests of apples.

Post Script
There can be no guarantees,
No ties of bondage;
All must be submitted in prayer,
All is subject to Divine Will.

Trust

Now you've read my thoughts,
And I stand naked before you,
Though *you* are still dressed for winter;
I feel no shame.
Peace fills my heart, mind and soul.

PART TWO

Words from the Depths of Sheol

The Perils of the Sea

Far farther out to sea
Than I can hope to swim unaided,
Swept out by my own stubbornness
And disbelief that I could slip,

I call for the Captain.
He hears me and turns, smiling kindly.
He himself throws down the life line,
I take it and he draws me close.

Nearer to the ship now,
Reassured of my deliverance,
I search one last time in the depths,
And release the rope, foolishly.

But the siren I glimpse
As I succumb to the downward pull,
Is not that creature of beauty,
But an unknown, menacing beast.

I call for my Master.
Undeserving, I watch him wrestle,
His flesh tearing, and his blood spilt
He lifts me, limp, to safety.

Resistance

I saw what was good;
Though grateful for answered prayers,
My soul tore apart.

Straddling two Worlds

I inhabit two worlds:
That of my condition,
Amid successful colleagues,
Where appearances and ambition
Reign supreme.
A veritable financial dream,
Vision of hell;
And a haven wherein dwell
Real friendships, and life's goal,
Self-expression,
A home for my soul.

Let Them Come, Part I

You'd think a God who cared
would reach out a helping hand,
having asked his child to rip out her own heart.
You'd think he'd give some small grace
to make it possible.
You'd think he'd allow some joy
for having done The Right Thing,
for saying "Let Your will not mine, be done."
But no such luck.
So let them come down,
these torrents of torment;
floods of frustration,
amid clouds of confusion
and the vile serpents of self-pity.
Let them come.

Expletives to Peace—
(an "ukiah-haiku")

Expletives explode!
My mind once an oasis,
now a battlefield.

****

Praises proclaim peace . . .
My mind, once a battlefield,
now an oasis.

One Week

One week, I was
wallowing in weakness,
with a wavering will.
Written words . . . whimsical words?
Would a wind
of wisdom
waft into my will?

Comment:
And I wasn't even twying to allitewate!

Shipwreck

It was plain sailing,
She was on the perfect tack;
He took her by storm,
Threw her completely off course,
Then abandoned ship; now wrecked.

Silence

Your silence tells me loud and clear
How you wish I wasn't here.
In love and war all is fair,
Which is why I'm able to declare
The truth is that you just don't care.

Strength in Weakness

I cling to you, Lord
With all my heart, mind and soul
Too dreadful not to.

The Angel

I never knew his name
But he was there for me
When no-one else was.
He stood by me,
Reading the words,
Watching silently.
They would have been my last sentences,
Written in the sand,
And soon to be washed away like their author.
But he stood over me,
Waiting calmly,
Knowing that I could not move
While he was there.
A time passed,
And still he stood,
Quietly,
Until finally, I got up and walked away.

My God, My God, Why have I Forsaken You?

I had placed my trust
In Man, who cannot be trusted,
Given my faith
To Man, who cannot be faithful,
Handed my heart
To Man, who cannot love,
And I saw that it was not good;
So I will place my trust
In You, who are Trustworthiness,
I will give my faith
To You, who are Faithfulness,
And Hand my heart
To You, who are Love.

Weakness and Strength

In weakness, there is disorder,
Confusion,
Insecurity, rivalry,
Obsessive behaviour,
Leading to guilt,
And fear of loss.

Desperation
Leads to submission
And prayer;
Prayer brings comfort
and strength.

In strength,
There is resolve and care taken
That no damage will be inflicted
On another's life mission,
No harm done to their loved ones,
Nor to their well-being,
Nor to their soul;
In strength, there is peace,
And gratitude
For every blessing.

PART THREE

Healing and Peace

A Morning Swim

Far farther out to sea
Than I have ever swum unaided,
In the sure knowledge of my safety,
I swam this morning.

Conscious of the presence of My Captain,
Knowing that I carry Him within me,
I swam,
Past rocks that threaten with their cragginess.
Over sea urchins much larger
Than I thought possible,
And swam,
Until my limbs
Could bear no more.

Turning onto my back,
And towards the cove,
I allowed His Spirit
to carry my limp body into shore.

Words of Comfort

My words of comfort,
Unappreciated, turn
Back to soothe my soul.
Finally some kindness
And understanding come my way,
Bringing healing in their path.

Love to the Loveless Shown

Will I forgive?
A childhood devoid of
Normality, affection,
Wearing to school a label
Bearing one word: "victim"
Inviting kicks and punches
From those who couldn't face
Their own battles at home.
Yes, I remember their names and faces,
And pray for them sometimes.
But do I forgive?

Mistaking for love,
Manipulation, repeatedly,
Until settling instead,
For a lack of vulnerability,
Ignoring the challenge
Of trying to grow a forest
Without a single seed;

Decades later,
Still faced with the jealousy
Of one whose sole vocation
Is to nurture,
Can I forgive?

Carving my own path of devastation
Into the hearts of those entrusted to me,
Will I stand on the ledge of unforgiveness,
Afraid to take a step in any direction,
Or will I cast off and with sweet praise,
Find that in spite of broken wings,
I can fly?

Profound Soul (as Affirmation)

I am God's masterpiece
To be celebrated,
Not a mistake,
To be crossed out.

The Creator wants me to live
As the best version
Of the wonderful person
He made me to be.

A profound soul,
He made no mistakes in me,
I was especially
and exquisitely designed,
To serve and to love.

All He asks of me
Is to give Him the glory,
Remaining ever faithful to Him;
And though I may be suffering now,
Eventually, I will
RADIATE TRUE JOY.

Words of Balm

These challenges are opportunities for growth.
The search is now on for what can be learned.
There is no resurrection without crucifixion,
But resurrection will come.

I have already learned
That the answer to everything is prayer,
I may not have the exact solution,
But I can put my hand in the hand of He who does,
And the other hand in that of our heavenly mother.
I must be patient with myself,
Life's lessons are a process,
And may take some time.
There is no need to beat myself up.
If I have done wrong,
I can confess it
To the one who will deliver and save.
He will cleanse and heal,
And resurrection will come.

I can speak with a holy Christian soul,
Trained in giving His Love
To broken ones.
Well-meaning friends
Can destroy
With their helpful ideas,
But no-one knows God's plans.
He is the God of creation,
Not destruction.

Though I have looked for solace
Where only destruction can be found,
I am called to build up not tear down.

I will look for Him
In oases of peace.
He is there,
Waiting to be found.
I will be still
And wait for renewal;
Then Resurrection will come.

I won't listen
To the negative voice
In my head.
It comes from the enemy
Of my soul.
He wants me to believe
That what's bad is good,
And what's good is bad.
I will pray for discernment
To know the difference.
I will trust the Lord,
And put everything in his hands.
He knows far better than I can
What is best for me
At any particular time.
The right path is impossible
To follow alone.
But all things are possible with God.
The joy of resurrection will come.

Blind Faith

I have a dream or vision,
which may cause you much derision,
that one day reality
may bring about an alteration
in my actuality.
Without hesitation,
you may claim
it's pure delusion,
but I choose to remain
in what you'd call confusion,
for my stubborn belief
is my only saving grace from grief.
You see, when I am praying,
I hear a voice, and it's saying:
"Be calm, and you will see,
if only you will trust in Me."

Dare to Hope, ask John . . .

As long as we *obey His commands*,
it seems we are allowed to make demands.
All we have to do is *bear fruit that will remain*,
and we will have no reason to complain,
for "Whatever you ask the Father in my name,"
Jesus said "He will give you,"
And yet some people say this isn't true.
But, "Ask and you will receive,
so that your joy may be complete."
If He didn't mean it,
why did He repeat and repeat
these words?

Biblical References:
John Ch 15, vs 7, vs 16; Ch 16, vs 23, vs 24

I Thirst

Words are of the greatest value
to every woman's heart,
Like sunlight and water
To a delicate flower,
Struggling to survive
In a tarmac lot.
They make ALL the difference,
Though the surroundings remain unchanged.
Who can honestly say they've never felt any comfort
from them?

I brought written words
Before the Lord,
I hardly know why,
Except there was a voice
As I was going through the door,
"Bring them into My Presence."
There must have been need
For further submission,
For giving back what belongs to Him.

Throw away the straw,
I cannot sip elegantly
From the chalice of His Love,
But sit, face upturned,
Mouth open wide,
Like a newly hatched chick;
Pour the lot over my head.
Drench me.

Let them Come, Part II

He gave them authority
To heal every disease and affliction
So I now call upon this,
As benediction;
He redeems our lives
From the depths of darkest hell
Gives sight to the blind,
Causes the sick to be well;
He was sent to free all the oppressed,
And to give good news
To those who are depressed;
He came that we
May have life abundantly,
So I say: "Let the rain of blessings
Come down on me."

There is Nothing Shallow

There is nothing shallow
About giving up your will
For another's sake.
It's not run of the mill,
But a harder path to take:
Struggling against emotion,
Holding firm to devotion,
Deciding to *not speak out*,
When you'd rather scream and shout,
Practising self-denial:
In fact, this is life's true trial.
There's nothing shallow about it,
No, nothing shallow at all.

Broken Instrument

The more broken the instrument,
The better the Master can use it;
The more insignificant the tool,
The greater the work.

So let's say "Yes" to abundance,
"Yes" to joy, "Yes" to compassion,
For along with admission
Of weakness and contemplation,
Compassion is all.

Like a Phoenix

What is my worth,
If I have no work?
Or my value,
When I'm a victim?
What is my purpose,"
When I'm falling apart?

They call this
"A season of growth,"
"Time to let go,"
To be alone,
With only my old friend, pain, for company.

No addiction can tempt me,
No self-harming, nor eating disorder;
No medication has power to save me.

I thirst for a single word of comfort,
Yet, none is offered,
Though I have spoken torrents of them to so many;

All I hold is an awareness of unmet needs,
And the satisfaction
Of making small changes,
In the knowledge that others are too
Overwhelming,
And must wait until another day,
To be faced.

And they will be faced.

I have the patience of a saint now,
And begin to know my worth,
Though it remains, as yet, unseen by others.

Misery can no longer drown me.
Instead, I pass through its flames,
Like a phoenix, patiently
Preparing for rebirth.

PART FOUR

Trust in the True Rock

Happiness is . . .

knowing that my life
is in the hands of one
whose ideas from above
are always based on love,
whose actions are constructive,
whereas mine are only self-destructive;
He has a boundless mind
and is infinitely kind.
He said, "Ask and you shall receive"
So why should I not believe?
And why should I ever fear,
when such a one is near?

In Heaven

I wonder if in Heaven,
we'll offer our arms
and legs to hungry mosquitoes, saying
"Have a drink, my dear."
After all, it is written
"the lamb will lie down with the lion*",
so why not?

*Biblical Reference: Isaiah 11, vs 6-9

Let them Come, Part III

Let them come:
too fat or too thin,
the tall, the short
and the ugly;
let them come.

The homeless,
the lonely and depressed,
the unemployed,
or *"failures" and social misfits,*
yes, let us come to the Lord.

Whether rich or poor,
learned or ignorant,
don't turn them away.

Let the old or infirm,
married, single or divorced,
all come to the Lord.

Let them all come.
Don't stop them;
let the children of the Lord
come unto Him.

Not Silence

It was not silence
That enveloped you,
Two thousand years ago
In Galilee,
But peace.

You heard the same sounds
That I hear now:
The barking of a distant dog,
The mistimed calling of a cockerel,
The snorting of a horse nearby.

But as you sit beside me,
Keeping me company in this starlit garden,
(So far from modern frenzy,)
I too am by your side,
That night in Gethsemane,
Waiting for what was to come.

A Thousand Praises

I'm counting my paces, *that's ten,*
Just jogging along, *making twenty,*
Inhaling a breath, *through thirty,*
Feeling a heartbeat, *at forty,*
Each breath bringing healing, *for fifty,*
Pumping and pulsing, *on sixty,*
Blood and abundance, *beats seventy,*
Exhaling unease, *to eighty,*
United with nature, *at ninety,*
Each set of *a hundred* repeated times ten,
A thousand praises to God!

Plans

Here was my plan, Lord,
But I submit to your will
So, what is your plan?

The Shack

I have a longing for a shack,
With a little wooden door,
I'd walk each morning down the track,
To Missionaries of the Poor.
Living there in such simplicity
Would bring the purest felicity,
Trusting that the Lord provides
And following what He decides.
I'd immerse myself in the care
Of the unloved, and in prayer,
Then drift into a peaceful sleep,
So replenishing and deep,
Knowing that I'd spent the day
In the most fulfilling way.

This Day

I had a hunch
I'd sing badly
On this day
Vegetable soup
Was all our lunch
On this day

By three-thirty
Head is spinning
On this day
Tempers are frayed
No-one winning
On this day

Strumming love songs
Brain pulsating
On this day
Conversations
Are frustrating
On this day

I fall asleep
Forget it all
On this day
My cell phone rings
"Sorry to call
On this day"

My blurry eyes
Can't find my tea
On this day
I find it then
Spill it on me
On this day

Panic sets in
I find a tiny tin
Of lobster paté of all things
And make scrambled eggs on toast
to somehow appease the demons that attack
On this day

Remnants of grey
On all our brows
Crosses that say
"Make Lenten vows"
On Ash Wednesday

Forgiveness

Not seven,
But seventy-seven times,
We are told;
An eternity of times.

There is nothing *you* can do,
To make amends.

Like love,
Forgiveness cannot be earned,
Or bought,
Only freely given,
Though undeserved.

Trusting

I'm trusting in God more and more
That he's providing for me every day,
That he is arranging things his way,
That even if he shuts a door,
He's opening a whole host more
Of little doors where I may enter
Without fear. He is the centre
And I'm praising,
Knowing that he answers prayers,
Handing him my precious cares,
And all the while, my heart is blazing.

Trust in the Rock

It's not for you to mock,
That I've tried to do God's will,
Put my trust in the Rock,
Taken a sour pill.

It was hard to swallow
But I'm carrying my cross.
I could easily wallow
In self-pity for my loss.

But the more I give glory,
The more I give praise,
He blesses my story
And enfolds all my days.

A Prayer for Today

Together we pray for ourselves,
For all those we love,
And for those we need to learn to love.
Lord, we ask that you would give us all healing
Wherever we need it.

Bless our minds and take from them
All negativity, and anything that is not of you.
Fill them with your thoughts
And right thinking.

Come now into our souls.
Purify them and guide them
To do your will and
Give glory only to you.
Bless our conversations
And every utterance from our mouths.

Lay your hands on our hearts
And set them free
From any unhealthy attachments.
Fill them with your love.
Thank you for showing us
How to love generously,
Without the condition
Of being loved back.

Thank you for our bodies.
Help us to see them as your Temples.
Though imperfect by the standards of the world,
Help us to accept and love them
Just as they are,
And to care for them as you ordained.

Help us to grow in faith,
Give glory to you in our work,
Give your love to others in holy relationships,
And learn to trust completely in you.

Glory and thanks be to
God the Father, Son and Holy Spirit,
That you are guiding us and teaching us,
In every situation.

We pray we will be more aware
That you are providing for us
And loving us each day.
Amen

Printed in the United States
By Bookmasters